Renewed by Jesus

My Guide to Reconciliation

Colin and Aimee MacIver

ASCENSION

West Chester, Pennsylvania

Nihil obstat:	Rev. Msgr. J. Brian Bransfield, STD
	Censor Librorum
	October 26, 2022
Imprimatur:	+Most Rev. Nelson J. Perez, DD
	Archbishop of Philadelphia
	November 2, 2022

Ascension
PO Box 1990
West Chester, PA 19380
1-800-376-0520
ascensionpress.com

Cover and interior design: Stella Ziegler, Sarah Stueve

Interior art: Mike Moyers, Stella Ziegler, Sarah Stueve. See additional illustration credits on page 92.

Printed in the United States of America

ISBN: 978-1-954881-77-8

Contents

RENEWED
My Guide to Reconciliation

My name is

_____

My church is

_____

The Ten Commandments

I.   I am the LORD your God: you shall not have strange gods before me.

II.   You shall not take the name of the LORD your God in vain.

III.   Remember to keep holy the LORD's Day.

IV.   Honor your father and your mother.

V.   You shall not kill.

VI.   You shall not commit adultery.

VII.   You shall not steal.

VIII.   You shall not bear false witness against your neighbor.

IX.   You shall not covet your neighbor's wife.

X.   You shall not covet your neighbor's goods.

The Beatitudes

Blessed are the poor in spirit, for theirs is the kingdom of heaven.

Blessed are those who mourn, for they will be comforted.

Blessed are the meek, for they will inherit the earth.

Blessed are those who hunger and thirst for righteousness, for they will be filled.

Blessed are the merciful, for they will receive mercy.

Blessed are the pure in heart, for they will see God.

Blessed are the peacemakers, for they will be called children of God.

Blessed are those who are persecuted for righteousness' sake, for theirs is the kingdom of heaven.

Introduction

YOU ARE MADE AND LOVED BY GOD. The most important things to remember throughout your entire life are that God loves you more than you know and that he wants you to be happy with him in heaven.

God knows that the only way for you to be happy throughout your life is by following his rules so you can eventually be with him forever in heaven. Like a good Father, even though he gives you rules to follow, he does not force you to follow them, because he wants you to learn how to make good choices on your own.

God made every person in this world, including you, with the ability to choose between right and wrong. Good choices help us to live our lives well. Bad choices are called sins. Every person struggles with sin. Sins are things we choose to do, not mistakes that happen by accident. Sin hurts us and others and pushes us away from God. God loves you so much. He never wants you to be hurting or far away from him, and knowing that we would sin, he had a plan from the beginning for our salvation.

God the Father sent his Son, Jesus, to live a human life, to die on the Cross, and to rise from the dead in order to save us from our sins. Forty days after his Resurrection, Jesus ascended to heaven. He did this in order to save us! God wants us to be happy with him forever.

The path to heaven can be hard. Sometimes we sin even though we know it is wrong. God knew we would struggle with sin. He gave us the Sacrament of Reconciliation to heal our souls from sin as often as we need.

The Sacrament of Reconciliation is a gift given to us by Jesus himself. In Matthew 18:18, Jesus says to his Apostles, "Truly, I say to you, whatever you bind on earth shall be bound in heaven, and whatever you loose on earth shall be loosed in heaven." Jesus gave his Apostles the power to forgive sins. Priests today have the power to forgive sins through apostolic succession and the power of Jesus Christ.

When you go to the Sacrament of Reconciliation, you may be worried about telling your sins to the priest. After all, these are the things you are most ashamed of! But don't worry. Priests are bound by the seal of Confession, which means they must keep anything they hear in Confession a secret—even if they're threatened with death! You do not have to fear going to Confession—the Sacrament of Reconciliation is there to heal you so you can be free to live your best life, the one Jesus calls you to live.

The Sacrament of Reconciliation heals us. Just like your body needs help to heal, so does your soul. Some sins are like spiritual scrapes and bruises. We call these spiritual bumps and bruises *venial sins*. Did you know that when you bless yourself with holy water or ask God's forgiveness at Mass, your soul can be healed from venial sins?

Other sins are more serious. These sins are called *mortal sins*. They are more than just bumps and bruises on our souls. They are like big spiritual injuries. Just as your body needs special help from a doctor for a bad injury, like a broken bone, your soul needs special help from a priest when you commit a mortal sin. The Sacrament of Reconciliation heals us from serious injuries to our souls. It also helps reconcile us to God, restoring sanctifying grace that is lost due to mortal sin.

It is true that venial sins and mortal sins hurt us. But the great news is that God loves to forgive and heal us. Jesus' sacrifice to save you defeated sin first. Every time you go to Confession, Jesus defeats sin again! Every time you go to Confession, you get closer to

God. The Sacrament of Reconciliation helps us stay on the path toward heaven. It is one of God's best gifts. This book will help you go to Confession and become the holy saint God wants you to be.

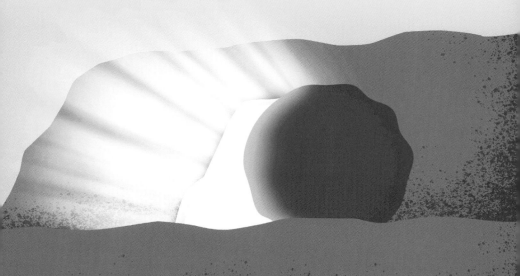

Sin Hurts Us, but Reconciliation Heals Us

Reconciliation means **"bringing back together."** The Sacrament of Reconciliation is God's gift to make us whole again when we sin. How does sin hurt us? How do we repair the hurt it causes?

What Makes a Sin?

Sins are our bad choices. Sins are not mistakes that happen by accident. When we do something that we know is wrong, we sin. Sin hurts us and others and pushes us away from God. All sins are choices against loving God and others.

There are a few signs that can help us to know if our choice is sinful. A choice is sinful if:

- It is a choice that we make (NOT something we do by accident).

- It is a choice to do something that God tells us not to do.

- It is a choice NOT to do something that God tells us to do.

- It is a choice that is bad for us and the people around us.

- It is a choice that pushes us away from God and heaven.

Here are some things that God gives us to help us learn right from wrong:

- **The Ten Commandments** show us how to live a happy, holy life.

- **The Catholic Church** teaches us about what is right and wrong.

- **Our parents** or other adults who take care of us teach us what is right and wrong. We can ask our parents for help when we aren't sure whether a choice is right or wrong.

- **Other trusted adults**, like priests and teachers, can also help us. We can ask them for help when we aren't sure whether a choice is right or wrong.

- **Our own consciences** help us know whether a choice is right or wrong. Your conscience is like a voice inside your heart that warns you when a choice is wrong. The older you get and the more you try to do good, the better your conscience will work.

The Types of Sin

There are many different things that can harm our bodies. Different problems need different kinds of care. Sometimes your body has a small cut that needs to be cleaned and covered with a bandage to heal. Other times, a bandage won't be enough. For more serious repairs, like stitches or surgery, you need to go to a doctor. There are also different kinds of problems or sins that can harm our souls. Different kinds of sin need different kinds of care.

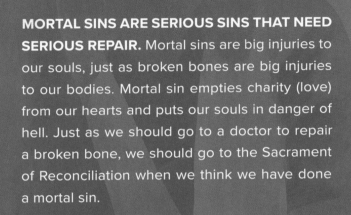

MORTAL SINS ARE SERIOUS SINS THAT NEED SERIOUS REPAIR. Mortal sins are big injuries to our souls, just as broken bones are big injuries to our bodies. Mortal sin empties charity (love) from our hearts and puts our souls in danger of hell. Just as we should go to a doctor to repair a broken bone, we should go to the Sacrament of Reconciliation when we think we have done a mortal sin.

THERE ARE THREE PARTS TO A MORTAL SIN.
A mortal sin can happen only if all three parts are done together:

1. A mortal sin goes against the Ten Commandments in a *serious* way. This is called *grave matter*.

2. A mortal sin is a sin that we *know* is very serious. This is called *full knowledge*. *Mortal sins cannot be done by accident.*

3. A mortal sin is a sin that we *freely choose* to do even though we know it is serious and wrong. This is called *full consent*.

How do I know it could be a mortal sin?

- Was it very serious?

- Did I know it was very serious?

- Did I choose to do it anyway?

- Go to Confession!

VENIAL SINS ARE SMALLER SINS. Venial sins are small injuries to our souls, just as cuts or bruises are small injuries to our bodies. Venial sins are not as serious as mortal sins, but they hurt us and others. They push us away from God. Even though venial sins are smaller than mortal sins, they still need repair. If we don't repair small cuts and bruises on our bodies, they can become infected and cause more harm. Our bodies become weak, and we are more likely to get sick in other ways. If we don't repair venial sins, our souls get weaker, and we are more likely to commit mortal sins. That's why it's important to go to Reconciliation often.

What Is Forgiveness?

God never wants us to be hurt or far away from him. He is happy when we are sorry for our sins and ask for forgiveness. God never gets tired of forgiving us! There is no sin, no matter how serious, that God will not forgive. Forgiveness is God healing us from our sin. God will always be disappointed by our sin, but instead of being angry or turning away from us, he offers us his love. This gift from God is called *mercy*.

Jesus tells us a story in the Bible about the prodigal son. The prodigal son leaves his father and chooses to do many serious sins. Afterwards, he is sorry and wants to go back to his father, but he thinks his sins might be too bad to be forgiven. But when the son comes back to apologize, his father runs to hug him and has a party to celebrate!

This is how God is with us. When we choose to sin, God is always waiting and hoping that we will come back to him.

How do we receive God's mercy? First, we trust that God loves us and wants to repair our souls from the hurt that sin causes. Next, we admit that we have sinned. We do not pretend that our sins were accidents or make excuses for our sins if we meant to do them (remember, accidents aren't sins). We admit the truth that we made a bad choice, and we are sorry; this is called *contrition*.

Jesus taught us that if we want God to forgive our sins, we must forgive others from our hearts. When we pray the Our Father, we ask God to "forgive us our trespasses as we forgive those who trespass against us." This means we must forgive others the way that we want God to forgive us. God forgives us as we forgive others. If we freely forgive others, God will freely forgive us.

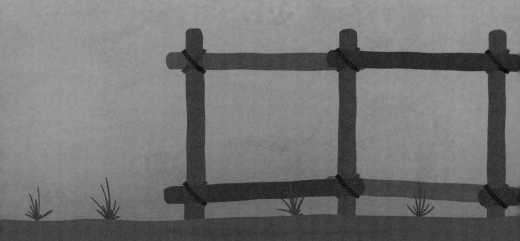

You and Your Conscience

We learn about the world around us by asking questions. When you were little, you probably pointed to things and asked, "What's that?" Part of your inner world is your *conscience*.

What Is a Conscience?

Your conscience is not a body part inside you, like a kidney or a liver. Your conscience is like a voice inside your mind and heart that tells you whether your choices are right or wrong. It can also help you see how and why you make the choices you do. The Holy Spirit helps lead your conscience. God gives us our consciences to help us know and choose good.

Your conscience can tell you about

- What you already did
- What you are doing
- What you are thinking about doing

Your conscience is like a pencil that needs to be sharpened. Following the Ten Commandments, praying, and listening to Jesus all sharpen your conscience. The older you get and the more you try to do good, the better your conscience will work.

Lax

When your conscience isn't sharp enough, it is called a *lax* conscience. A lax conscience doesn't care whether choices are right or wrong. It is like a pencil that has no point. It doesn't work very well. A lax conscience makes excuses for sin, like "Everyone else is doing this" or "I just really want to do this."

Scrupulosity

When your conscience is too sharp, this is called *scrupulosity*. A scrupulous conscience is afraid that everything is a sin, even things we do by accident. It is like a pencil that has a point that is so sharp, it keeps snapping. God wants us to take sin seriously because sin hurts us, but God does not want us to be afraid that everything we do is a sin.

What Is an Examination of Conscience?

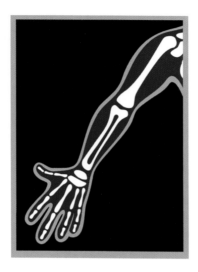

An **examination** is a deep look into something. Doctors do examinations, or exams, on patients to see what is wrong with their bodies. Exams help doctors give patients the correct treatment to heal their bodies. Confession is healing for our souls. Before we go to Confession, an exam of our choices shows us how we need to ask for forgiveness from God.

An *examination of conscience* is a deep look at our choices. We think about what we have done and why we did it. This helps us know our sins so we can ask God to forgive us and heal our souls. Remember that we must confess mortal sins to repair the serious injury they do. We should also confess venial sins so that our souls do not become weak.

Remember: Jesus Is a Friend

When you examine your conscience, remember a few important things:

- Accidents are not sins. Sins are choices we know are bad and choose to do anyway.

- Confession is about Jesus setting us free from sin because he loves us! We should be sorry for our sins. We should see how much sin hurts us and others. But we should also have joy because God wants to heal us.

- Confession heals our relationship with Jesus. Jesus is your best friend who wants to be close to you!

How to Go to Confession

You have learned a lot about how sin hurts us and how God repairs us in Confession. God loves you so much and never wants you to be hurt or far away from him. When we are sincerely sorry for our sins and ask for his forgiveness, God forgives us. What good news! Do not be afraid to let God heal your soul. Let's go to Confession!

BEFORE CONFESSION

It's okay to be nervous before Confession. Remember that God is happy you are going to Confession. He wants you to be reconciled to him. In your heart, thank God for his love and mercy.

Now, find a place to be quiet and still. Choose an examination of conscience from the back of this book to help you examine your soul.

Next, follow the directions where you are. Most people make a line and take turns. You can ask someone

if you don't know where to line up. While you wait for your turn, ask the Holy Spirit to help you make a good Confession.

You can go to Confession either face-to-face with the priest or behind a screen. Either way is good. Pick the way you like best. Sometimes there are different lines for the two ways. You can ask someone if you don't know which line to pick.

CONFESSION BEGINS

The priest will start Confession. He will make the Sign of the Cross to begin. He may also say hello.

Then you will say,

> *Bless me, Father, for I have sinned. It has been [length of time] since my last Confession. These are my sins.*

Tell the priest the last time you went to Confession. If you don't remember exactly, just do your best. For example, you can say, "about one month" or "a few weeks." If you don't remember at all, that's okay! You can say, "I don't remember when my last Confession was."

If this is your first Confession, say,

> *Bless me, Father, for I have sinned.*
> *This is my first Confession.*

> *Name your sins*

Name all the sins you can remember, big and small. Do not skip any sins on purpose. Remember that God loves you and will forgive every sin you name. Some people make a list to help them remember all the sins they want to confess (make sure you get rid of it after you're done).

COUNSEL AND PENANCE

When you finish naming your sins, you can say,

> *These are all my sins.*

or

> *For these and all my sins,*
> *I am very sorry.*

The priest may talk to you about how to avoid sin after Confession. He will then give you a *penance*. A penance is some action to repair your soul from sin. It is an outward expression of the sorrow we feel for our sin and something to help us right the wrong we have done. The penance helps with the effects of sin and helps us to be free to love God and detached from our sins. Most penances are prayers or small actions. We must do our penance for Confession to be complete. You should try to do your penance right after you leave Confession.

ACT OF CONTRITION

The priest will ask you to pray an Act of Contrition. This is a prayer that tells God you are sorry for your sins and asks for his forgiveness. You can pray the Act of Contrition below or the traditional version on page 80. If you forget the words, it's okay! You can ask the priest to help you.

> *My God, I am sorry for my sins with all my heart. In choosing to do wrong and failing to do good, I have sinned against you whom I should love above all things. I firmly intend, with your help, to do penance, to sin no more, and to avoid whatever leads me to sin. Our Savior Jesus Christ suffered and died for us. In his Name, my God, have mercy. Amen.*

ABSOLUTION

The priest will now offer *absolution*. This is the moment God forgives your sins. After this prayer and your penance, your sins are forgiven! What a special moment. God loves you so much. He is so happy to forgive you.

> ### HERE ARE THE BEAUTIFUL
> ### WORDS OF ABSOLUTION:
>
> *God, the Father of mercies, through the death and resurrection of his Son, has reconciled the world to himself and sent the Holy Spirit among us for the forgiveness of sins; through the ministry of the Church, may God give you pardon and peace, and I absolve you from your sins in the name of the Father, and of the Son, and of the Holy Spirit. Amen.*

The priest will end by blessing you: "In the name of the Father, and of the Son, and of the Holy Spirit."

Make the Sign of the Cross as he blesses you.

You can thank the priest for hearing your confession and then exit the confessional.

AFTER CONFESSION

YOU ARE FORGIVEN! You may feel excited. You may feel normal. Forgiveness does not depend on your feelings. No matter how you feel, God has forgiven you. If you can, stay in the church to do your penance. It is best to do your penance right away so you don't forget. While you pray, thank God for his mercy.

HOW TO GO TO CONFESSION:
QUICK GUIDE

- The priest welcomes you.

- Make the Sign of the Cross and say, **"Bless me, Father, for I have sinned. It's been [length of time] since my last Confession."**

- **Name all your sins**, big and small. Do not skip any sins on purpose.

- The priest gives you advice, a penance, and asks you to pray an **Act of Contrition** (see page 31 or 80).

- The priest says the words of absolution, and God forgives your sins!

- Make the Sign of the Cross while the priest blesses you.

- Say, **"Thank you, Father!"** and exit.

- Pray your penance right away.

- Thank God for the gift of Reconciliation and for his mercy.

This is how we make the Sign of the Cross

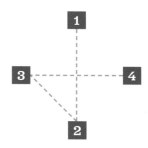

1	2	3	4
In the Name of the Father	*and of the Son*	*and of the Holy*	*Spirit.*

With your right hand, touch your forehead.	Touch your chest.	Touch your left shoulder.	Touch your right shoulder.

 Amen.

Praying in God's Mercy

Along with going to Confession, we can pray to learn about God's mercy. Here are some prayers to help you think about and receive God's mercy.

Holy Water

At Mass there are many ways we ask for God's mercy and learn to forgive others. When we enter the church and bless ourselves with holy water, we remember our baptism. At Baptism, God washed away our sins and made us his children.

The Sign of the Cross

In the Name of the Father, and of the Son, and of the Holy Spirit.

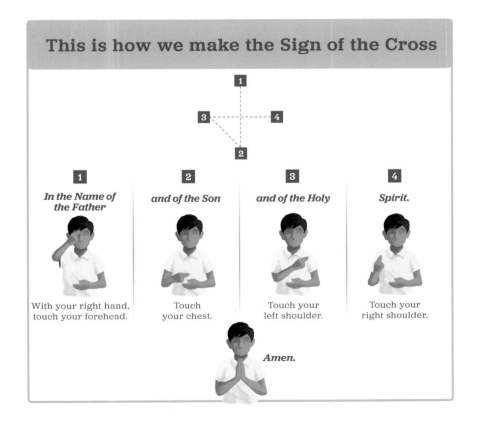

This is how we make the Sign of the Cross

1
In the Name of the Father

With your right hand, touch your forehead.

2
and of the Son

Touch your chest.

3
and of the Holy

Touch your left shoulder.

4
Spirit.

Touch your right shoulder.

Amen.

The *Confiteor*

In this prayer, we tell God we are sorry for our sins and ask him to forgive us.

I confess to almighty God

and to you, my brothers and sisters,

that I have greatly sinned,

in my thoughts and in my words,

in what I have done

and in what I have failed to do,

through my fault, through my fault,

through my most grievous fault;

therefore I ask blessed Mary ever-Virgin,

all the Angels and Saints,

and you, my brothers and sisters,

to pray for me to the Lord our God.

The Our Father

Jesus told us how to pray to God the Father. God is happy when we pray because it shows that we trust him. We praise God for being so good. We ask God to give us what we need. God will always do what is best for us. We also ask God to forgive us and help us avoid sin. This prayer reminds us of God's mercy.

Our Father, who art in heaven,

hallowed be thy name;

thy kingdom come,

thy will be done

on earth as it is in heaven.

Give us this day our daily bread,

and forgive us our trespasses,

as we forgive those who trespass against us;

and lead us not into temptation,

but deliver us from evil.

The Sign of Peace

The sign of peace reminds us that God's people are a family. We should love everyone like we love our own families. This is a way we reconcile with and give mercy to others.

Priest: The peace of the Lord be with you always.

YOU: *And with your spirit.*

Priest: Let us offer each other a sign of peace.

**Give the people near you a sign of peace
(for example, a handshake or a wave).**

The Chaplet of Divine Mercy

Jesus gave this simple and powerful prayer to St. Faustina and asked her to share it with the world. Use your rosary to pray it.

The Divine Mercy Chaplet is a special prayer for God's mercy. Jesus taught it to St. Faustina. Like the Rosary, the chaplet is very easy to learn if someone shows you how the first few times and prays it with you.

We use ordinary rosary beads for the Chaplet. We begin with the Sign of the Cross, one Our Father, one Hail Mary, and the Apostles' Creed.

On each Our Father bead, pray:

Eternal Father, I offer you the Body
and Blood, Soul and Divinity
of your dearly beloved Son,
our Lord Jesus Christ,
in atonement for our sins and
those of the whole world.

On each Hail Mary bead, pray:

For the sake of his sorrowful Passion,
have mercy on us and on the whole world.

Repeat these prayers on each decade. When you finish the fifth decade, you will be back on the centerpiece. Finish the chaplet by praying these words three times:

Holy God, Holy Mighty One,
Holy Immortal One,
have mercy on us
and on the whole world.

Close with the Sign of the Cross.

Living in God's Mercy

God has called you to an important mission: to bring his mercy into the world. The **corporal and spiritual works of mercy** are ways you can answer this call! The corporal works of mercy are ways to help people with their needs on earth. The spiritual works of mercy are ways to help people get to heaven.

STRENGTHS:

Feeds the hungry

Gives drink to the thirsty

Clothes the naked

Shelters the homeless

Visits the sick

Visits prisoners

Buries the dead

SPECIALTY:
Corporal Works of Mercy

Corporal Works of Mercy

Spiritual Works of Mercy

SUPERKID PROFILE #2646

STRENGTHS:

Instructs the ignorant

Counsels the doubtful

Admonishes sinners

Bears wrongs patiently

Forgives offenses willingly

Comforts the afflicted

Prays for the living and the dead

SPECIALTY:

Spiritual Works of Mercy

Examining
Your Conscience

How to Make a
Good Examination
of Conscience and Confession

1. Find a place to be quiet and still.

2. Choose an examination of conscience from the back of this book to help you.

3. Ask the Holy Spirit to help you.

4. Think about your choices. Think about what you have done wrong. Think about what you should have done but did not do.

5. Use the Ten Commandments to remember what God tells us we should do and should not do.

6. Use the Beatitudes to remember how Jesus told us to live.

7. Go to Confession. Do not be afraid. Ask for God's forgiveness. Remember that God loves to forgive you and heal your soul!

Examination of Conscience from the

TEN COMMANDMENTS

God gives us the Ten Commandments to show us how to live a happy, holy life. The Ten Commandments tell us what we should do and should not do. Ask the Holy Spirit to help you see any way that you did not keep the Ten Commandments.

First Commandment: "I am the LORD your God: you shall not have strange gods before me."

○ Did I try to make God the most important thing in my life?

○ Did I act like other things, activities, or people are more important than God?

○ Did I spend time with God each day in prayer?

○ Did I thank God for the good things he has given me?

○ Did I receive Holy Communion with mortal sins that I have not confessed yet?

Second Commandment: "You shall not take the name of the LORD your God in vain."

O   Did I always use God's name with love and respect?

O   Did I use God's name out of anger or as a curse?

O   Did I speak badly about God, the saints, or any other holy person or thing?

O   Did I use bad language or curse words?

Third Commandment: "Remember to keep holy the LORD's Day."

O   Did I miss Mass on Sunday or a holy day of obligation on purpose without a good reason (like being sick or not having a ride)?

O   Did I complain about going to Mass?

O   Did I pay attention at Mass as well as I could? Did I say the responses, pray, and sing?

O   Did I fast (no food or drink except water) for one hour before receiving Holy Communion?

O   Did I rest on Sundays?

Fourth Commandment: "Honor your father and your mother."

O   Did I show love and respect to my parents or the adults who take care of me?

O   Did I disobey them? Did I get angry or talk back to them?

O   Did I try to be thankful for what my parents do for me?

O   Did I help my family at home? Did I complain about chores?

O   Did I argue or fight with my brothers or sisters? Am I kind to them?

O   Did I respect and obey other adults in charge (priests, nuns, teachers, police, etc.)?

O   Did I obey the rules at school?

O   Did I do my best on homework and other schoolwork?

Fifth Commandment: "You shall not kill."

O   Did I hurt anyone on purpose?

O   Did I make fun of others or call them names?

O   Did I lose my temper or get angry at anyone?

O   Did I not forgive someone?

O   Did I leave out anyone on purpose?

O   Did I talk badly about others or gossip?

O   Did I share what I can with others, especially those who have less than I do?

O   Did I try to take care of my body?

Sixth and Ninth Commandments: "You shall not commit adultery." "You shall not covet your neighbor's wife."

O   Did I try to treat my body and others' bodies with respect?

O   Did I think about disrespectful things on purpose?

O   Did I listen to or tell disrespectful jokes?

O   Did I look at disrespectful images, videos, TV shows, or movies?

Seventh and Tenth Commandments: "You shall not steal." "You shall not covet your neighbor's goods."

o   Did I steal anything?

o   Did I take something without permission? Did I purposely not return something?

o   Did I damage someone else's things?

o   Was I greedy or selfish?

o   Did I share what I can, especially with those who have less than I do?

o   Am I thankful for what I have?

o   Am I jealous of what others have or what they can do?

Eighth Commandment: "You shall not bear false witness against your neighbor."

O Did I lie? Did I tell half the truth?

O Did I blame others for something that I did?

O Did I spread rumors about someone?

O Did I tell secrets?

O Did I cheat on schoolwork or in a game?

O Did I keep my promises?

O Did I keep silent when I should have said something?

Examination of Conscience from the

BEATITUDES

God wants you to have a happy, holy life. Sin hurts our chances of happiness. The Ten Commandments tell us what we should do and should not do in our actions. Sin can also be in our hearts and minds. Jesus gave us the Beatitudes to show us how to use our minds and hearts. Ask the Holy Spirit to help you see any way you did not follow the Beatitudes.

"Blessed are the poor in spirit, for theirs is the kingdom of heaven."

O Did I try to keep God as the most important thing in my life?

O Did I act like other things, activities, or people are more important than God?

O Did I spend time with God each day in prayer?

O Did I thank God for the good things he has given me?

O Did I steal anything?

O Did I damage someone else's things?

O Was I greedy or selfish?

O Did I share what I could, especially with those who have less than I do?

O Did I try to be thankful for what I have?

O Was I jealous of what others have or what they can do?

"Blessed are those who mourn, for they will be comforted."

O   Did I ignore someone who needed help or comfort on purpose?

O   Did I try not to complain?

O   Did I try to be kind to people who are hurting?

O   Am I sorry for my sins?

O   Did I try to repair how my sins hurt others?

O   Did I apologize and ask forgiveness if I did something wrong?

O   Did I do nothing when I should have helped?

"Blessed are the meek, for they will inherit the earth."

O   Did I try to get my own way instead of thinking about others?

O   Did I hurt someone on purpose?

O   Did I make fun of others or call them names?

O   Did I lose my temper or get angry at anyone?

O   Did I talk badly about others or gossip?

O   Did I use bad language or curse words?

O   Did I refuse to forgive someone?

O   Do I treat others with respect?

O   Did I leave anyone out on purpose?

"Blessed are those who hunger and thirst for righteousness, for they will be filled."

O   Is God the most important thing in my life?

O   Did I always use God's name with love and respect?

O   Did I miss Mass on Sunday or a holy day of obligation on purpose without a good reason (like being sick or not having a ride)?

O   Did I complain about going to Mass? Did I listen to my parents when they asked me to get ready?

O   Did I pay attention at Mass? Did I say the responses, pray, and sing?

O   Did I keep Sunday as a day of rest by avoiding work I didn't need to do?

O   Did I try my best not to sin and ask God for help?

O   Did I keep silent when I should have said something?

"Blessed are the merciful, for they will receive mercy."

○ Did I try to get even with someone who hurt me?

○ Did I think badly about someone on purpose?

○ Did I not forgive someone?

○ Did I show love and mercy to others?

○ Did I try to help others when I could?

○ Did I try to think about others more than about myself?

"Blessed are the pure in heart, for they will see God."

O   Did I treat my body and others' bodies with respect?

O   Did I think about disrespectful things on purpose?

O   Did I listen to or tell disrespectful jokes?

O   Did I look at disrespectful images, videos, TV shows, or movies?

O   Did I cheat on schoolwork or in a game?

O   Did I lie? Did I tell half the truth?

O   Did I spread rumors about someone?

"Blessed are the peacemakers, for they will be called children of God."

O Did I apologize and ask forgiveness if I did something wrong?

O Did I try to repair how my sins hurt others?

O Did I try to help others get along? Or did I try to make others upset with each other?

O Did I lose my temper or get angry at anyone?

O Did I hurt anyone on purpose?

O Did I show love and respect to my parents or the adults who take care of me?

O Did I disobey them? Did I get angry or talk back to them?

O Did I help my family at home? Did I complain about chores?

O Did I argue or fight with my brothers or sisters? Am I kind to them?

O Did I respect and obey other adults in charge (priests, nuns, teachers, police, etc.)?

"Blessed are those who are persecuted for righteousness' sake, for theirs is the kingdom of heaven."

O   Did I show that I love Jesus, even if people make fun of me?

O   Did I try to do what God wants more than what I want?

O   Did I listen to my conscience? Or did I ignore my conscience?

O   Did I follow others telling me to do something wrong?

O   Did I stand up for what is right, even if people made fun of me?

O   Did I try to forgive others who hurt me? Did I pray for them?

O   Did I defend people who get bullied or treated unfairly?

O   Did I try to offer up my suffering to God instead of complaining?

Examination of Conscience from the

SEVEN DEADLY SINS

The seven deadly sins are serious sins. They are big injuries to our souls. They are all ways of being selfish instead of loving.

Pride

is thinking we are more important
than anyone else.

O   Did I try to show off?

O   Did I act like a know-it-all?

O   Did I brag on purpose?

O   Was I happy when someone else made
    a mistake?

O   Did I laugh or make fun when someone
    else got in trouble?

Envy

is being upset when something good
happens to someone else.

O   Did I get upset when something good
     happened to someone else?

O   Did I get angry that I did not get the
     same thing as others?

O   Did I complain when someone had
     something that I did not?

O   Did I enjoy it when others lost
     something good?

O   Am I jealous of what others have or what
     they can do?

Lust

is using others instead of loving them.

O   Did I use someone just to get something from them?

O   Did I try to get others to do something wrong?

O   Did I treat my body and others' bodies with respect?

O   Did I think about disrespectful things on purpose?

O   Did I listen to or tell disrespectful jokes?

O   Did I look at disrespectful images, videos, TV shows, or movies?

Wrath

is being more angry than we should
be or trying to get even.

O   Did I hate anyone?

O   Did I try to hurt anyone on purpose?

O   Did I try to get even with someone who
hurt me?

O   Did I think badly about someone on purpose?

O   Did I not forgive someone?

Greed

is being selfish with our things and not thankful for what we have.

O Did I steal anything?

O Did I take something without permission?

O Did I purposely not return something?

O Was I greedy?

O Did I always want more than what I have?

O Did I share what I can, especially with those who have less than me?

O Am I thankful for what I have?

Sloth

is being lazy and not helpful.

O   Did I help my family at home? Did I complain about chores?

O   Did I try to help others when I can?

O   Did I do nothing when I should have helped?

Gluttony

is taking too much of something, especially things that are not good for our bodies.

O   Did I take more than my share of something?

O   Did I waste something on purpose?

O   Did I try to take care of my body?

Prayers to Know

Traditional Act of Contrition

O my God, I am heartily sorry for having offended thee, and I detest all my sins because I dread the loss of heaven and the pains of hell, but most of all because they offend thee, my God, who are all good and deserving of all my love. I firmly resolve, with the help of thy grace, to confess my sins, to do penance, and to amend my life. Amen.

Our Father

Our Father, who art in heaven,

hallowed be thy name;

thy kingdom come,

thy will be done

on earth as it is in heaven.

Give us this day our daily bread,

and forgive us our trespasses,

as we forgive those who

trespass against us;

and lead us not into temptation,

but deliver us from evil.

Amen.

Hail Mary

Hail Mary, full of grace,
the Lord is with thee.
Blessed art thou among
women, and blessed is the
fruit of thy womb, Jesus.
Holy Mary, Mother of God,
pray for us sinners now and
at the hour of our death.
Amen.

Glory Be

Glory be to the Father and to
the Son and to the Holy Spirit,
as it was in the beginning,
is now, and ever shall be,
world without end. Amen.

St. Michael Prayer

St. Michael the Archangel,
defend us in battle.
Be our protection against the
wickedness and snares of the devil.
May God rebuke him, we
humbly pray. And do thou,
O Prince of the heavenly host,
by the power of God,
cast into hell Satan and
all the evil spirits
who prowl through the world
seeking the ruin of souls.
Amen.

St. Faustina and the Ocean of Mercy

Once there was a nun named Sr. Faustina. She loved Jesus very much. Then a miracle happened–Jesus began to appear to her and talk to her! Sr. Faustina told her spiritual director that she was seeing visions of Jesus, but her spiritual director didn't believe her. He said, "If Jesus is really appearing to you, ask him to tell you the last sin I confessed." So the next time Jesus appeared to Sr. Faustina, she asked him what the priest's last confessed sin was. Jesus replied, "I do not remember. All the sins confessed are thrown into the ocean of my mercy."

Whenever you go to Confession, you can be sure that Jesus forgives your sin. In fact, Jesus doesn't even remember it. He no longer sees your sin; he only sees you, his beloved child. Your sins are gone forever in the ocean of his mercy. Alleluia!

Illustration Credits

The following works are reprinted by permission from the Student Workbooks for *Renewed: Your Journey to Reconciliation* and *Received: Your Journey to Holy Communion* © 2023 Ascension Publishing Group, LLC:

81   *The Shepherd and the Ninety-Nine Sheep* by Mike Moyers

83   *Jesus Welcoming the Children* by Vicki Shuck

85   *Mary, the Mother of God* by Liz Blair

87   Image from BibleBox

89   *St. Michael's Battle* by Chris Lewis, Baritus Catholic Illustration

91   *St. Maria Faustina Kowalska* by Liz Blair

Meet the Authors

Colin and Aimee MacIver are a husband-and-wife team who have been teaching, writing, and ministering together for more than twenty years. They are also parents who have learned many powerful lessons from their children.

When their son completed his first Reconciliation, he said, "My heart is free! Thank you, Jesus, for forgiving my sins!" When their daughter prepared for her first Communion, she asked, "Is Jesus wearing a bread costume?" Children have a true gift for teaching adults about God's wonder and beauty.

Colin and Aimee have coauthored several resources about the sacraments, including *Belonging: Baptism in the Family of God*; *Chosen: Your Journey Toward Confirmation*; *Connected: Catholic Social Teaching for This Generation*; and *Power and Grace: Your Guide to the Catholic Sacraments*.